Glimmers in the Mystic Mist

In the dawn, a whisper calls,
Softly through the veils it falls.
Golden rays through fog entwine,
Nature's breath, a sacred sign.

Footsteps hush on dew-kissed grass,
Secrets hide where shadows pass.
Leaves that dance with gentle grace,
Spirit forms in this embrace.

Echoes of Midnight Miracles

Stars ignite the velvet night,
Dreams take flight in silver light.
Time stands still as shadows play,
Whispers of the night delay.

Laughter soft, like distant chimes,
Caught in moments, held in rhymes.
Every breath a promise made,
In the dark, fears start to fade.

Luminous Reflections on Still Waters

Beneath the moon, the waters gleam,
Rippling softly, like a dream.
Secrets stirred in tranquil flow,
Mysteries the waters know.

Capturing the essence bright,
Of the stars that grace the night.
A quiet world, in silence deep,
Where the heart can rest and leap.

Gentle Flickers in the Sylvan Grove

In the woods where soft winds sigh,
Fireflies dance 'neath the twilight sky.
Branches sway with a tender ease,
Nature hums a lullaby, please.

Colors blend as dusk descends,
Every shadow, a friend extends.
Whispers weave through leaves above,
Cradling the echoes of love.

Celestial Gleams in Stillness

In twilight's hush, the stars awake,
Soft glimmers dance on the silver lake.
Whispers of night in the cool, crisp air,
Dreams take flight like the shadows that dare.

Golden rays of the waning sun,
Fade into dusk, the day is done,
Nature holds secrets in its embrace,
Where silence thrives, and time leaves no trace.

Beneath the veil of a starlit sky,
Mysteries linger as night draws nigh.
Among the leaves, a gentle sigh,
Echoes softly as the world passes by.

With every breath, the stillness grows,
A tapestry woven from the night's prose.
In this sacred space, we find our peace,
As the celestial gleams never cease.

Luminous Whispers from the Sylvan Realm

In tangled woods where the shadows play,
Murmurs of magic chase the day.
Leaves rustle softly, secrets unfold,
Stories of nature patiently told.

Moonbeams slip through the branches wide,
Painting the ground where the fairies hide.
With every flicker, a promise shines,
In the heart of the forest, love entwines.

Luminous whispers, a soft refrain,
Cascading echoes of joy and pain.
Deep in the woods, life finds its song,
Where every heartbeat knows it belongs.

Ancient trees, guardians so wise,
Keep watch under the starlit skies.
In shadows cast by the glowing light,
The sylvan realm breathes with pure delight.

Glimmers in the Moonlit Glade

In the glade where moonlight spills,
Glimmers dance on the tranquil hills.
Silver threads weave through the night,
Binding together the dark and the light.

A gentle breeze stirs the leaves above,
Whispers sweet as a heart in love.
Glowing fireflies flit and play,
Guiding lost souls along their way.

Here in the stillness, magic grows,
In the soft glow where serenity flows.
Every shadow tells a tale,
In the moonlit glade where dreams prevail.

With every step on the mossy ground,
The beauty of night is ever profound.
Glimmers of hope in the dark we see,
Under the gaze of the old oak tree.

The Gentle Rise of Mystic Radiance

As dawn approaches, the shadows wane,
A gentle rise of light through the rain.
Mystic radiance paints the skies,
Bringing warmth where the heart lies.

Hues of lavender and softest gold,
Unfold like stories that never grow old.
With each new dawn, the world awakes,
Forging paths with the choices it makes.

In the heart of morn, the silence breaks,
Nature's symphony, the earth it quakes.
Tiny birds chirp a sweet refrain,
Heralding the day in a joyous gain.

The rise of light brings forth new dreams,
As rivers flow with golden beams.
In the embrace of warmth and grace,
Mystic radiance finds its place.

Hums of Life Beneath the Canopy

In the forest's heart, where shadows play,
Gentle whispers blend with the day.
Leaves flutter softly, secrets unfold,
Nature's story, vibrant and bold.

Roots intertwine, a dance so deep,
Life's hidden wonders, ours to keep.
Birdsongs echo, a melodious tune,
Under the gaze of a sleepy moon.

Streams babble tales of ages past,
Moments fleeting, yet meant to last.
Critters scurry, in light and in shade,
Underneath the boughs of emerald glade.

Sunlight dapples, in patches bright,
Filling the woods with warmth and light.
Every rustle and gentle sigh,
A reminder of life that passes by.

Subtle Flames of Hidden Hope

In the quiet dusk, embers glint,
Flickers of dreams where shadows hint.
A heart that's weary, yet holds the flame,
Finding its strength, refusing to wane.

A whisper of courage, soft and clear,
In the darkest moments, hope draws near.
Stars in the sky, like promises bright,
Guiding the lost through the fabric of night.

Warmth of a smile, a tender embrace,
Tales of survival etched in each face.
Life's journey unfolds, like chapters unwritten,
In the silence, connections are smitten.

When fears threaten to dim the spark,
Remember the light that flourishes in dark.
Each flicker a signal, love's gentle art,
Subtle flames igniting the bravest heart.

Whispering Wishes in Moonlit Air

Beneath the moon's glow, the world takes a breath,
Each sigh of the night, a promise of death.
Wish upon stars that twinkle so bright,
In the hush of the moment, find solace tonight.

Echoes of laughter, shadows at play,
Moments entwined, in twilight's ballet.
Dreams take flight on the wings of the breeze,
Carried aloft, with effortless ease.

Magic of night, where fantasies soar,
Every heartbeat speaks of wanting more.
Whispers of wishes, secrets untold,
Entwine in the air, more precious than gold.

With each silver beam that races the dawn,
A tapestry woven with hope reborn.
In the stillness, find dreams that inspire,
Whispers of wishes, igniting the fire.

Ethereal Rays on Enchanted Paths

On ethereal paths where light softly weaves,
Nature unveils its wonders and leaves.
Each step taken, a dance of delight,
Guided by rays that shimmer in flight.

Through the tangled woods, secrets lie deep,
Where shadows awaken, and night takes a leap.
A flicker of light in the thicket's embrace,
Calling out gently, inviting our trace.

Moss cushions the ground, a carpet of dreams,
Where sunlight breaks free and softly redeems.
Colors burst forth in a radiant song,
An invitation to wander, to belong.

Winding through groves with an aura so bright,
Ethereal beauty enchants the night.
Every moment a gift, the journey our own,
Paths steeped in magic, together we're shown.

The Stillness of Hidden Wonders

In the hush of the night air,
Secrets softly lay bare.
Whispers of dreams in repose,
Nature's heart gently glows.

Shadows weave a tapestry fine,
Starlight dances, divine.
Hidden gems in the dark,
Awakening each quiet spark.

Beneath the moon's tender gaze,
Time slows, the world stays.
Each beat of silence profound,
In this stillness, hope is found.

Echoes of life softly sigh,
As the night drifts on by.
In the calm, wonders appear,
Filling the heart with cheer.

In twilight's embrace, we rest,
In this stillness, we feel blessed.
The world turns, yet here we stay,
In the stillness, come what may.

Calls of the Ethereal Evening

As daylight fades into the night,
The sky dons a starry sight.
Whispers echo through the trees,
Carried softly on the breeze.

Cascading shadows come alive,
In this quiet, spirits thrive.
Crickets sing their lullaby,
Underneath the velvet sky.

Moonbeams glisten on the ground,
Magic stirs all around.
Time drifts like a gentle stream,
Granting life to each sweet dream.

Celestial voices call us near,
Filling hearts with love and cheer.
In this moment, we belong,
Guided by the evening's song.

An ethereal dance begins to play,
We lose ourselves, night becomes day.
Underneath the stars, we roam,
Finding in evening's arms our home.

Memories Wrapped in Shimmering Veils

In whispers soft, the past unfolds,
Woven in threads of silken gold.
Faded echoes in the air,
A tapestry beyond compare.

Each moment a precious gem,
Time recalls where we have been,
Wrapped in dreams both bright and pale,
Life's stories in shimmering veil.

Fragments dance with gentle grace,
Reflecting light upon each face.
Moments cherished, never lost,
In the heart, worth any cost.

Through the haze of memory's glow,
Forgotten paths begin to show.
In these veils, we often find,
The treasure that life left behind.

Wrapped in love, we journey on,
With every heartbeat, a new dawn.
Through shimmering veils, we shall see,
The beauty of what's meant to be.

Silhouettes of Fable Underneath Starlight

In the twilight, tales ignite,
Casting silhouettes in the night.
Stories told in shadows deep,
Awakening dreams from their sleep.

Underneath the heavens wide,
Fables etch as the stars collide.
Figures dance in graceful arcs,
Painting magic, leaving marks.

Whispers of lore float through the air,
Ancient themes, beyond compare.
Each silhouette, a life once lived,
Holding secrets yet to give.

In the charm of this night's embrace,
Every shadow finds its place.
Through the dark, we find our way,
Guided by the night's ballet.

So let us dream 'neath the starry glow,
With each fable, let our spirits grow.
In shadows deep, we find our flight,
In silhouettes of the endless night.

Whispers in the Moonlit Glade

The trees sway gently, secrets shared,
In shadows deep, our hearts laid bare.
The moonlight dances on the ground,
In whispers soft, lost dreams are found.

A breeze carries tales of old,
Of lovers' vows, in night so bold.
Stars above softly gleam and glow,
In this glade, our spirits flow.

The nightingale sings a haunting tune,
A serenade to the lonely moon.
Each rustling leaf, a story told,
In the silver light, our fears unfold.

Footsteps echo on the mossy floor,
As echoes linger, forevermore.
The world outside fades to a hum,
In the glade, our hearts become one.

With every whisper, magic weaves,
In the tranquil night, the heart believes.
As dawn approaches, shadows fade,
But love remains in the moonlit glade.

Fading Embers of Enchanted Dreams

In twilight's glow, the embers spark,
Whispers of magic in the dark.
Once vivid colors begin to wane,
Leaving echoes of a soft refrain.

Dreams that danced in fervent light,
Now flicker softly, dimming bright.
Yet in the hush, a promise stirs,
Enchanting tales the silence purrs.

Beneath the stars, we used to sigh,
While shadows played and spirits flew high.
Now fading glimpses haunt the night,
Of stolen dreams that took to flight.

The coals still glimmer, though slight they seem,
Holding the warmth of our lost dream.
In every shadow, a memory gleams,
Holding tight to fading dreams.

Through twilight's door, the magic ebbs,
But in our hearts, the story webs.
For though embers fade into night,
In dreams, we will always find light.

Silvery Threads of Forgotten Lore

In ancient woods where shadows play,
Silvery threads weave night and day.
Echoes of laughter, lost in time,
Lingering softly like whispered rhyme.

Each leaf a page of tales untold,
Secrets buried, treasures bold.
Under the sky so vast and wide,
Forgotten lore, a timeless guide.

The brook hums softly, a calming tune,
Beneath the watchful, patient moon.
Stories of old dance in the breeze,
In every rustle, knowledge frees.

As twilight falls, the stars ignite,
Guiding us gently through the night.
In silken whispers, we are drawn,
To shadows where the past goes on.

With every step, we hear the call,
Of spirits vibrant, enthralling all.
In the embrace of nature's core,
We find the threads of everlasting lore.

Beneath the Serene Canopy

Beneath the trees, where shadows blend,
A soothing silence, hearts mend.
The canopy whispers, secrets spread,
Cradling thoughts, where worries tread.

Sun-drenched leaves cast patterns bright,
Bathed in a warm, golden light.
Nature breathes in calming sighs,
Beneath her watchful, gentle eyes.

A symphony of rustling leaves,
In harmony, the spirit weaves.
Each creature stirs in tranquil peace,
Beneath the boughs, our cares release.

The world outside feels far away,
In the stillness, we long to stay.
As moments linger, time stands still,
A sanctum found within the will.

Together we find solace here,
In bonds of laughter, love, and cheer.
Beneath this serene, enchanted dome,
At nature's heart, we find our home.

Flickers of History in Nature's Grasp

In the rustle of leaves,
Whispers of tales unfurl,
Echoes of ages past,
Nature's memory in twirls.

Through the branches of time,
Stories dance in the breeze,
Each flicker a moment,
Captured in the trees.

Rivers carve ancient paths,
Mountains hold secrets tight,
Witness to the passing,
Of day turning to night.

Footsteps caught in shadows,
Footprints on the ground,
Nature keeps our stories,
In silence, profound.

With every sunset glow,
History finds its voice,
In the flickers of light,
Nature's timeless choice.

Twilight Serenades on Soft Echoes

As day meets the night,
The horizon blushes deep,
Whispers of twilight sing,
In shadows, secrets creep.

Stars begin to shimmer,
In a velvet expanse,
Moonlight weaves a tale,
Of a silent romance.

The nightingale's song,
Wraps the world in its charm,
Soft echoes of the heart,
A soothing, gentle balm.

Clouds drift like whispers,
Over valleys and hills,
Each note is a promise,
As the evening stills.

In the hush of the dusk,
Magic fills the air,
Twilight serenades call,
Inviting us to share.

A Brush of Magic in the Mundane

In the clatter of cups,
Amid morning's soft light,
Magic brews in silence,
Transforming day from night.

A stroll down the street,
Where shadows play and gleam,
Every glance a treasure,
Every smile a dream.

Life's simplest moments,
Like petals softly fall,
Hold a brush of wonder,
In the grand, hidden hall.

In the rust of old gates,
Or the dawn's gentle rise,
Magic swirls in plain sight,
If we choose to be wise.

With a heart wide open,
To the world all around,
Every day holds beauty,
In the lost and found.

Whispers of Old Souls in Nature

Beneath the ancient trees,
Where roots intertwine,
Old souls share their stories,
Interwoven, divine.

The babbling brook sings,
Of moments long since gone,
Every drop a memory,
In the dawn's soft dawn.

The mountains stand guard,
In their wisdom, so grand,
Whispers of old souls,
On this blessed land.

Birds, like messengers,
Carry tales through the skies,
Nature's breaths so gentle,
Hold the truth that never lies.

In the rustle of grass,
Where the wildflowers bloom,
The spirit of the ancients,
Lingers in the room.

Tranquil Moments on Still Waters

Gentle ripples caress the shore,
Whispers of peace fill the air.
Reflections shimmer, soft and pure,
Nature's calm, beyond compare.

Willows sway in the breath of dusk,
Crickets sing in evening's embrace.
Beneath the stars, the world feels hushed,
Time drifts slowly, a warm embrace.

The moonlight dances on the lake,
A silver veil, delicate and bright.
Each moment shared, a cherished take,
In solitude, everything feels right.

A boat floats gently on the stream,
With every stroke, the heart beats slow.
Dreams are woven in quiet dream,
As nature's lullaby starts to flow.

In these moments, life feels clear,
The mind finds rest, the spirit soars.
Beneath the night, there's naught to fear,
These tranquil waters hold open doors.

Glints of Wonder in the Dappled Light

Sunlight filters through emerald leaves,
Casting shadows on the ground.
A tapestry of gold that weaves,
Magic lies in nature found.

Breezes whisper secrets untold,
As petals dance upon the breeze.
In each glint, a story unfolds,
Invitation to take a moment to seize.

The land awakens with vibrant hues,
Colors play in joyous delight.
From morning's dawn to evening's blues,
Summer's warmth shines ever bright.

Each glimmer speaks of days gone by,
Memories held in the heart's embrace.
In dappled light, we pause and sigh,
Finding solace in this sacred space.

With each step, wonder greets the soul,
In the forest where dreams ignite.
Here, beneath the trees, we feel whole,
In glints of wonder, pure and right.

Soft Glows of Twilight Reverie

Twilight descends in gentle hues,
Softly painting the evening's face.
As daylight fades, time softly cues,
A world wrapped in a warm embrace.

Whispers of night sing to the stars,
Each sigh a secret, softly shared.
The horizon glows with hopes from afar,
As day surrenders, unprepared.

The air is thick with dreams to weave,
Underneath the violet sky.
In this hour, our spirits believe,
As shadows stretch and softly sigh.

Candles flicker, casting soft light,
A hearth aglow with love's sweet grace.
In quiet moments, hearts take flight,
In twilight's arms, we find our place.

Here in reverie, thoughts take shape,
As night whispers promises anew.
In soft glows, we escape the drape,
Of worries dimmed, with evening's view.

The Dance of Stars on Velvet Skies

In the stillness of a midnight sea,
Stars awaken, twinkling bright.
A dance of dreams, wild and free,
Painting the dark with their light.

Velvet skies hold tales of old,
Ancient stories written in fire.
Each light a wish, a heart's true bold,
In this sphere, we chase desire.

Constellations speak in whispers low,
Guiding lost souls through the night.
A celestial map, mysterious glow,
In the vastness, stars gleam with might.

Comets drift in a graceful sweep,
Woven paths from time's own hand.
In their trails, our secrets keep,
A universe vast, beyond land.

So let us dance under the night's reign,
As the stars twirl in cosmic grace.
In their light, we find joy and pain,
In the dance of hearts, in this infinite space.

Echoes of Serenity in Timeless Spaces

In quiet nooks where shadows play,
The silence speaks in gentle sway.
Whispers of dreams, softly unfurl,
As time drifts by in a tranquil whirl.

Beneath the sky, a canvas wide,
Where thoughts of peace and hope abide.
Each breath a song, a soothing balm,
In spaces still, the world feels calm.

Moments linger like morning dew,
A tapestry in varying hue.
Echoes dance on sapphire air,
Serenity found, beyond compare.

In every heartbeat, a promise clear,
To cherish now, hold memories dear.
Through endless paths, in twilight's light,
We find our way, through day to night.

Amongst the stars, we silently trace,
The essence of love and warm embrace.
In timeless realms, our spirits soar,
Echoes of peace forevermore.

The Soft Embrace of Wandering Spirits

In valleys deep, where shadows flow,
Wandering hearts begin to glow.
Through silent paths, they lightly tread,
In search of dreams that softly spread.

A gentle breeze carries their name,
Whispers of hope, igniting the flame.
Through tangled woods and silver streams,
They weave together forgotten dreams.

Each breath a tale of days gone by,
Where laughter rings and spirits sigh.
In twilight's arms, they find their way,
A dance of shadows, night turns to day.

United hearts in soft embrace,
Recall the warmth of time and space.
Like stardust sprinkled in the night,
They journey forth, embraced by light.

With every step, they leave a trace,
In the fabric of this sacred place.
Wandering spirits, forever free,
In the embrace of eternity.

A Dance of Flickers Through the Leaves

A flicker glints in emerald skies,
Where sunlight twirls and softly lies.
Dancing shadows weave and play,
Through the leaves, they find their way.

With every gust, the whispers flow,
An ethereal ballet set to slow.
Leaves applaud in rustling cheer,
As the world turns, the path is clear.

In golden hues, the seasons change,
Life's pirouette, sweet and strange.
Nature's chorus sings with grace,
In the arms of time, we find our place.

The breeze carries secrets, soft and sweet,
In every flicker, a heartbeat's beat.
United in rhythm, they twirl around,
In this dance of life, love is found.

Through the leaves, their stories wind,
A legacy of thoughts combined.
In every flicker, memories weave,
A dance of life that we believe.

Veins of Light Beneath the Forest's Skin

Beneath the bark, a secret glows,
Veins of light where magic flows.
In stillness deep, the whispers call,
As shadows roam and soft leaves fall.

In twilight's breath, the world unfolds,
Stories whispered, softly told.
Through tangled roots, the heartbeats hum,
The forest sings, a sacred drum.

Each pulse of light, a journey shared,
In nature's grip, our souls repaired.
A symphony of green and gold,
Carving paths through tales of old.

The canopy above, a woven lace,
Hiding dreams in a tranquil space.
Veins of light, in harmony thrive,
Guiding wanderers, fully alive.

With every step, they find the thread,
In the forest's arms, where wonders spread.
Veins of light beneath the skin,
A world anew, where life begins.

The Gentle Hug of a Silver Night

Underneath the starry skies,
Moonlight dances, softly sighs.
Whispers float on breezy wings,
Nature's hush, a lull that clings.

Shadows play in silver hues,
Glimmers spark as dreams infuse.
Sleep descends on weary eyes,
Wrapped in warmth, the world complies.

Branches sway with tender grace,
Echoes linger, time won't race.
Each heartbeat, a soothing balm,
In the night, we find our calm.

Crickets sing their lullaby,
As we watch the clouds drift by.
With every breath, the world feels right,
In the glow of a silver night.

Here in peace, our worries cease,
A gentle hug, a soft release.
Beneath the stars, our spirits soar,
In this embrace, we long for more.

Sleep of the Light in the Glade

Sunlight filters through the leaves,
Whispered dreams in soft reprieves.
In the glade where shadows play,
Time stands still, and hearts delay.

Golden rays on dewdrops gleam,
Nature's canvas, a quiet dream.
Amid the ferns, our spirits blend,
In this light, our worries mend.

Melodies of streams align,
With the rustle of pine and vine.
Cradled in the soft embrace,
Of the glade, a sacred space.

Gentle breezes weave their way,
Through the trees, they dance and sway.
In the warmth, we find our peace,
In this haven, joys increase.

Let us linger, let us rest,
In the light, we feel so blessed.
Sleep of the day, a tender shade,
In the glade, our hearts parade.

Vows of the Forgotten Breeze

Among the leaves, a promise flows,
Carried whispers where no one knows.
Time has painted tales untold,
In the breeze, a song of old.

Gently brushing against the skin,
Memories of where we've been.
Each sigh tells of love and loss,
Vows linger, despite the cost.

Through the fields of swaying grass,
Echoes of the moments pass.
Tangled roots and distant skies,
In the breeze, forever lies.

Silent oaths in rustling trees,
Softly laughed away by these.
Yet their essence, pure and free,
Kisses each soul with sweet decree.

Let us whisper to the night,
As the breeze takes flight.
Weaving stories, old yet new,
Vows of breezes, holding true.

Glows of a Lost Eden

Hidden realms in twilight's grace,
Echoes of a fabled place.
Where the rivers softly gleam,
And the skies hold dreams supreme.

Petal whispers brush the air,
Fleeting glows that linger there.
In the garden, time stands still,
Every moment holds a thrill.

Stars above in twilight dance,
Painting shadows in their trance.
Each leaf tells a tale of yore,
In lost Eden, evermore.

Joyous laughter weaves the night,
In the glow, we find our light.
Beneath the boughs, we seek our grace,
In this dream, we find our place.

Though the world may drift away,
In this Eden, we shall stay.
Glows of magic fill the skies,
In our hearts, forever rise.

Traces of Magic in the Quiet Sphere

In whispers of dusk, the shadows sway,
A dance of dreams, where silence lay.
Soft echoes weave through twilight's veil,
Where hopes are born, and voices pale.

Beneath the stars, the secrets gleam,
In gentle night, we lose our theme.
The moonlight bathes the earth in gold,
A tender story, yet untold.

With rustling leaves, the magic stirs,
In hidden paths, where nature purrs.
Each step we take, a sacred rite,
Awakening wonders, lost to sight.

A flicker here, a shadow there,
The world ignites in lovers' glare.
We reach for stars, for light anew,
In quiet spheres, where spirits flew.

A Symphony of Soft Rhythms

In morning's hush, the world awakes,
A symphony of love it makes.
With gentle winds, the trees now hum,
A melody where heartbeats drum.

Below the skies, where soft winds blow,
Flowing notes like rivers slow.
Each fluttering leaf, a songbird's plea,
In every sound, a memory.

The raindrops fall, a rhythmic beat,
As nature's choir sings so sweet.
With every drop, a story flows,
In harmony, the spirit grows.

The twilight blush, a softer hue,
Unfolds its charms, a gift so true.
In every pulse, in every sigh,
A symphony that fills the sky.

Glowing Dreams in the Heart of Nature

In forests deep, where shadows play,
Glowing dreams ignite the day.
Each whispering breeze, a secret told,
In nature's heart, where magic's bold.

The streams reflect the stars above,
A gentle pulse of peace and love.
With every step, the wild unfolds,
A tapestry of life so bold.

From mountain peaks to valleys wide,
The glowing dreams, our hearts confide.
In every bloom, a tale we weave,
In nature's arms, we dare believe.

With moonlit paths and sunlit streams,
We wander through our glowing dreams.
A world embraced by tender light,
In nature's heart, our spirits height.

Whirlwinds of Starlit Moments

In midnight's grasp, the starlight spins,
Whirlwinds of moments, where magic begins.
Each breath we take, a heartbeat shared,
In timeless dance, where none have dared.

With laughter bright, and shadows deep,
We chase the dreams that softly seep.
Through winding paths of endless night,
We find our way by starlit light.

The cosmos swirls, a bright cascade,
In the vastness, our fears fade.
We twirl and spin, in graceful flight,
Chasing the whispers of the night.

In every glance, a spark ignites,
Each moment captured, pure delights.
In whirlwinds of joy, we lose control,
Starlit moments that fill the soul.

A Flicker of Wonder in the Evening Shade

In twilight's grasp, shadows blend,
Whispers dance where dreams suspend.
Stars awaken, soft and bright,
Guiding hearts through deepening night.

Leaves rustle secrets, tales untold,
Each glimmering spark, a story bold.
Time drips gently, like honey's flow,
Where wonders bloom, and soft winds blow.

Underneath the arching sky,
Hope is woven, never shy.
Every flicker holds a wish,
Caught in the evening's tender swish.

The moonlight bathes the earth in grace,
A tender light, a warm embrace.
Moments linger, sweet and rare,
Echoing softly through the evening air.

As shadows stretch and whispers fade,
We find solace in the shade.
For in the stillness, hearts reside,
Cradled close, where dreams abide.

Threads of Light in the Mysterious Wood

In the heart of the ancient grove,
Sunbeams weave, a lace glove.
Branches twist like thoughts anew,
In whispers soft, they call to you.

Moss carpets paths of emerald hue,
Hidden stories in each dew.
Footsteps linger, dreams awake,
Awash in wonders, hearts will quake.

Silence sings a haunting tune,
Beneath the watchful, silver moon.
Each flicker, a secret shared,
In the wood, where hearts are bared.

The air is thick with tales of old,
Of adventure and courage, brave and bold.
In shadows deep, mysteries gleam,
We find ourselves within the dream.

As day yields to the velvet night,
Threads of light ignite our sight.
In the woods, let spirits rise,
For in the dark, our truth defies.

A Tapestry of Dreams and Whispers

In the fabric of night, dreams entwine,
Stitching together fate's design.
Whispers float on gentle breezes,
Carrying hopes, where heart seizes.

Stars are needles, sharp and bright,
Sewing tales in the velvet night.
Each spark a wish, each sigh a thread,
In this hushed world, where shadows spread.

Moonbeams shimmer, soft and clear,
Painting visions, drawing near.
In every corner, secrets sleep,
Cradled softly, within the deep.

Tales of joy, of love once lost,
Woven tightly, without cost.
A tapestry rich with history,
Unraveling life's grand mystery.

As dawn approaches, colors fade,
Yet in our hearts, we're not dismayed.
For dreams persist, in woven light,
Guiding us through the lingering night.

Flickering Will-o'-the-Wisps of Memory

In twilight's glow, memories flare,
Will-o'-the-wisps dance through the air.
Haunting echoes of laughter bright,
Guide lost souls in the soft twilight.

Fleeting visions, a soft caress,
Chasing shadows, we must confess.
In the mist, familiar faces shine,
Flickering softly, like olden wine.

Each glimmer a story, lost yet near,
Whispers of love, and traces of fear.
Through the dark, they light the way,
Reminding us of yesterday.

As shadows weave the fabric tight,
Fraying edges of day and night.
Our hearts remember, still and true,
The flicker's glow—ever anew.

In the quiet, let them soar,
These gentle wisps we can't ignore.
For in each flicker lies the key,
To the eternal dance of memory.

Shimmering Shadows in Still Waters

Beneath the trees, the stillness glows,
Reflections dance where the soft breeze blows.
Whispers of night, a gentle embrace,
Shadows entwine, in a shimmering space.

Stars shimmer bright on the water's face,
A mirrored world, a tranquil place.
Each ripple tells tales of ages gone,
In secret depths, the magic's drawn.

The moon sails softly, a silver light,
Guiding the dreams that take their flight.
In still waters, the heart finds peace,
As shimmering shadows whisper release.

Here echoes linger, stories decay,
In the night's embrace, we drift away.
The dance of shadows, soft and sweet,
In shimmering depths, our souls will meet.

Tranquil Flames of the Enchanted Woods

In the heart of the woods, where spirits convene,
Tranquil flames flicker, a magical scene.
Embers glow softly, a warm gentle light,
Embracing the silence of the deep night.

Fairy whispers float on the breeze,
Carving out dreams among ancient trees.
The flames draw nearer, like welcoming friends,
A solace found where the enchantment blends.

Granite stones hold the warmth of the fire,
In this sacred space, our hearts inspire.
Every flicker tells a tale untold,
In tranquil flames, our spirits unfold.

Night wraps around us, a soft velvet cloak,
As laughter mingles with the smoke.
In the enchanted woods, we carve our names,
With tranquil flames that hold our claims.

Murmurs of Light among Ancient Trees

Among ancient trees, soft murmurs rise,
Carried by winds beneath sprawling skies.
The light filters through, a golden beam,
In whispered secrets, we find our dream.

Each leaf a story, each branch a guide,
In the heart of the woods, where mysteries hide.
Echoes of laughter weave in the air,
Murmurs of light, a moment to share.

Golden shadows paint the forest floor,
Footsteps follow, forevermore.
In the stillness, our spirits ignite,
As we wander lost in whispers of light.

Timeless and gentle, nature's refrain,
Murmurs of love in the softest lane.
The trees stand tall, wise in their grace,
Guiding our journey to a sacred place.

Secrets of the Glowing Pathway

On the path aglow with secrets untold,
A journey unfolds, each step turns bold.
The light weaves through the branches above,
Whispering tales of magic and love.

With every footfall, a story is spun,
In shadows and light, we feel the sun.
The pathway sings with a soft, sweet tone,
Guiding the wanderers, not alone.

Glowing embers sparkle in the night,
Drawing us deeper into their light.
In the heart of the forest, dreams will awake,
With secrets hidden, for our hearts' sake.

As we tread softly on this radiant ground,
In each gentle whisper, the universe sounds.
The glowing pathway winds ever on,
In the dance of the night, till the dawn is drawn.

Whispers of Glimmering Threads

In the quiet of the night, they weave,
Shimmering tales that none believe.
Softly stitched with dreams untold,
Glowing secrets gently unfold.

Silver strands in shadows play,
Guiding souls who lost their way.
Each whisper dances through the air,
Knitting hopes with tender care.

Stars above twinkle with grace,
As if to join this hidden space.
Fingers grasp the precious light,
Crafting warmth from the cool night.

In every thread, a story's spun,
A tapestry where hearts are won.
Echoes linger, deep and sweet,
Drawing together what's bittersweet.

So listen close, as night descends,
To the dances that the fabric sends.
Whispers faint but ever bright,
Glimmering softly in the night.

Echoes Beneath the Starry Veil

Beneath the canopy of night,
Echoes pulse in silver light.
A whisper here, a sigh somewhere,
Secrets tangled in the air.

Stars like lanterns guide our dreams,
Flowing softly in moonlit streams.
Each twinkle tells of tales embraced,
In the quiet, we find our place.

Time stands still, the world at rest,
Hearts aligned, the soul's behest.
Breath of night, a sweet refrain,
Washing over like gentle rain.

In the stillness, visions soar,
As starlight opens every door.
What lies hidden, shy and small,
Awakes beneath the heavens' call.

And thus we dance, in shadows play,
Echoes leading our hearts away.
Underneath the starry veil,
We share secrets in the pale.

Flickers of Enchantment in Twilight Breeze

As daylight fades, colors blend,
Whispers of magic softly send.
Twilight dances, shadows grow,
In the breeze, secrets flow.

Glimmers shine like distant stars,
Painting dreams of who we are.
Each flicker holds a fleeting glance,
A chance to dream, a wisp of chance.

The air hums with vibrant tones,
Calling softly, a world of bones.
Here and there, the spirits play,
In flickers bright, night meets day.

Moments drift like leaves in flight,
Carried forth by gentle night.
A lullaby sways in the trees,
Enchantment whispers in the breeze.

So let us linger, let us chase,
Flickers lighting up this place.
In twilight's arms, we find our ease,
Dancing through this wondrous breeze.

The Serene Dance of Hidden Flames

In silent spaces, shadows glide,
Where hidden flames begin to bide.
A gentle warmth that stirs the night,
Holds the promise of soft light.

Within the dark, a flicker brews,
Ember whispers, soft and true.
Hearts entwined in tender sway,
Igniting love in the light of day.

Each step a rhythm, graceful flow,
A dance that only souls may know.
Flames leap high, then slowly wane,
Yet always born of sweet refrain.

Moments flicker, cherished bright,
Guiding paths through the velvet night.
In this warmth, we find our place,
In the embrace of time and space.

So let us dance, unseen, unbound,
With hidden flames where love is found.
A serene waltz, a sacred space,
In the hearts where we interlace.

Elusive Lights in the Nightshade

Whispers dance beneath the moon,
Shadows stretch, the night a tune.
Stars flicker, secrets they confide,
In dreams where hopes and fears collide.

Glimmers wink from hidden glades,
Floating softly, like serenades.
Each glow a story from afar,
Guiding hearts like a wandering star.

Doubts are cast in midnight's veil,
As courage weaves a delicate trail.
In the maze where shadows play,
Elusive lights will lead the way.

Echoes linger in silent spaces,
Time unfolds in gentle traces.
Nightshade cloaks all that we find,
In stillness, visions intertwine.

Awake to find the dawn's embrace,
Yet memories of the night we chase.
Fleeting joys in twilight's flight,
Forever lost in elusive light.

In the Embrace of Silver Hushes

Crickets chirp a lullaby,
Moonlight drapes the night, so shy.
Trees sway gently in the breeze,
As time slows down and hearts find ease.

Silver whispers softly sound,
In stillness, magic can be found.
Nature cradles every sigh,
In the embrace of night's lullaby.

Stars adorn a velvet dome,
Each twinkle sings us softly home.
In quiet waves of silver light,
We drift away, free from the fight.

Shadows dance in silhouette,
Memories linger, we won't forget.
In this world where silence reigns,
Our dreams awaken, free from chains.

As dawn approaches, shadows wane,
Yet in our hearts, remains the same.
The silver hush will ever call,
In memory's grasp, we hold it all.

Paths Untaken by Flickering Lights

Along the way where shadows tread,
Flickering lights like dreams unsaid.
Whispers lead to roads unknown,
In the twilight, choices are sown.

Footsteps echo through the night,
Each path a story, a chance for flight.
Beneath the stars, hopes intertwine,
In quiet moments, destinies align.

Some trails are wide, some narrow lie,
Curiosity stirs as spirits fly.
Yet each flicker calls to the brave,
To journey forth, our souls, we save.

With every turn, uncertainty's near,
But hearts ignited know no fear.
Flickering lights, a guiding spark,
Illuminating dreams that mend the dark.

As night retreats, our choices bloom,
Paths untaken dispel all gloom.
In every step, in every sigh,
The flickering lights, our spirits fly.

Dreamweaving in the Dappled Shade

Amidst the trees where sunbeams play,
Dreams are spun in a dappled sway.
Gentle sighs in warm embrace,
Nature's canvas, a sacred space.

Whispers linger on the air,
Promises held with tender care.
Beneath the boughs where shadows blend,
Every moment, a story penned.

In this realm where visions blend,
Night's enchantment, a faithful friend.
With every ray that filters down,
Resilient dreams, like flowers, crown.

Dappled shade, a soft retreat,
Cradles heartbeats to their beat.
Every sigh a wish takes flight,
In the stillness of the night.

As stars emerge and twilight glows,
Dreamweaving where the rivers flow.
In every shadow, in every light,
Life's gentle magic ignites the night.

Secrets in the Twilight Breeze

Whispers dance on evening air,
As shadows twine with fading light.
Secrets linger everywhere,
In twilight's gentle, soft delight.

Stars awaken, one by one,
As fireflies weave their glowing thread.
Night's embrace has just begun,
While dreams unfold and silence spreads.

The breeze carries stories near,
Of moments lost and joy regained.
Within each sigh, a note appears,
Of laughter shared, of love unfeigned.

Hidden realms beneath the night,
Where fantasies and truths collide.
In this place, hearts take their flight,
And all our fears and doubts subside.

So let us stroll through dusky trails,
With every step, a treasure found.
In secrets spun in twilight veils,
We leave our worries unbound.

Petals of Light on Whispering Winds

Softly falls the morning dew,
As petals dance on zephyr's breath.
Light cascades in golden hue,
Awakening the world from rest.

In gardens lush with colors bright,
Each bloom a tale of hope and cheer.
The whispers of the winds unite,
In harmony, all hearts draw near.

Sunbeams kiss the fragrant air,
As nature's symphony resounds.
Echoes of our dreams laid bare,
In every rustle, joy abounds.

Through the fields where wildflowers sway,
We chase the light, our spirits soar.
In every moment, we find play,
As whispers weave forevermore.

With each gust, new wonders gleam,
And laughter mingles with the breeze.
In petals' dance, we reign supreme,
Bound by love and timeless ease.

Veils of Dawn in the Woodland Realm

Morning breaks with subtle grace,
Where sunlight filters through the trees.
In the woodland's warm embrace,
Nature hums with tranquil ease.

Mist unfurls like silken threads,
As dew-kissed ferns begin to rise.
In this haven, worry sheds,
Awakening to clear blue skies.

Birdsongs weave a joyful tune,
As paths of wonder come alive.
In the cradle of the noon,
We feel the pulse of life revive.

Underneath the ancient boughs,
Where every whisper holds a tale,
In harmony, our spirits rouse,
While peace comes drifting on the trail.

Veils of dawn softly unfold,
In this realm where dreams are spun.
In nature's arms, we are consoled,
As day begins, our hearts are won.

Flickering Shadows of Lost Memories

Flickering lights in the dusk of time,
Shadows play on the fading wall.
Memories dance with a silent rhyme,
As echoes whisper, softly call.

Faces fade in the twilight glow,
Each moment held in fleeting hands.
A bittersweet, nostalgic flow,
Like footprints left on golden sands.

In silences, the past resides,
Where laughter lingers in the air.
Though time takes flight, the love abides,
In heart's embrace, forever there.

Waves of longing, softly crash,
As we reminisce by the shore.
With each flicker, memories flash,
A tapestry of love, and more.

So let us cherish every spark,
In shadows cast by yesterdays.
For though the night may loom quite dark,
Our hearts hold light in countless ways.

Ethereal Echoes of Nature's Embrace

Whispers dance on gentle breeze,
Softly weaving through the trees.
Leaves murmur secrets of the night,
Nature's pulse, a heartbeat's light.

Crickets serenade the moon,
As shadows sway to nature's tune.
Stars twinkle in the velvet sky,
A celestial lullaby does sigh.

Streams reflect the silver glow,
Carried softly, where wildflowers grow.
Petals shimmer in twilight's grace,
In this quiet, sacred space.

Misty trails of evening's kiss,
Whisper tales of nature's bliss.
In this realm where spirits play,
Echoes linger, night and day.

Each soft rustle and gentle sound,
Binds us to the earth's profound.
In every leaf and every sigh,
Nature's bond shall never die.

Starlit Secrets of the Hidden Meadow

In a meadow draped in night,
Stars weave tales in pure delight.
Moonbeams fall like silver threads,
Awakening dreams in sleepy heads.

Whispers float on winds so light,
Telling stories of the night.
Beneath the boughs of ancient trees,
Nature hums its melodies.

Fireflies blink with fleeting grace,
Dancing in their glowing lace.
Each secret shared in shimmering hue,
Brings the darkness life anew.

The nightingale sings, soft and clear,
With every note, the world draws near.
In this hidden, sacred glade,
All of nature's wonders played.

When dawn breaks with gentle blush,
The meadow stirs from evening's hush.
Secrets sleep 'til night returns,
In the starlit heart, the meadow yearns.

Glowing Traces of the Unseen World

Mists arise from forest floors,
Hidden realms behind closed doors.
In the shadows, spirits tread,
Where the path of dreams is led.

Glowing traces light the way,
Through the night where secrets stay.
Ancient echoes softly speak,
To the hearts that dare to seek.

A flickering light, a whispered sigh,
Hints of worlds not seen by eye.
Roots entwined with stories old,
Tales of magic yet untold.

Crystals glisten in the dark,
Each a wish, each a spark.
In the quiet, all is learned,
In the silence, spirits churned.

As the night begins to fade,
Awake the wonders that were made.
In the dawn's embrace, behold,
Traces of the unseen world, bold.

Mystic Lumens Beneath the Eldertree

Beneath the boughs of elder's grace,
A world of magic finds its place.
Whispers echo, soft and low,
As ancient roots in silence grow.

Lumens flicker in the night,
Guiding souls with their gentle light.
Each heartbeat thrum, a timeless song,
In this haven, we belong.

Fungi glow with colors rare,
Painting dreams upon the air.
Cradled in this twilight dance,
Nature beckons, take a chance.

As shadows stretch and stories weave,
The elder tree's heart gently breathes.
In its arms, every whisper is found,
Mystic lore of the earth profound.

So linger here, where time stands still,
In twilight's warmth, in night's goodwill.
Beneath the elder, join the flow,
Of mystic lumens, softly aglow.

Ethereal Flickers in the Forest Night

In the hush of night, they gleam,
Tiny lights dance, a whispered dream.
Stars bow low, reflecting grace,
Ethereal flickers in a secret place.

Moonbeams weave through ancient trees,
Mystic tales carried by the breeze.
Shadows flirt with soft delight,
In the heart of the forest night.

Crickets sing a gentle song,
Their melodies where spirits belong.
A world enchanted, dressed in dark,
Finding wonder in every spark.

Mossy stones beneath my feet,
Faintly glowing, a pulse so sweet.
Guiding paths in twilight's glow,
A celestial dance that ebbs and flows.

Whispers linger, secrets shared,
In this space, I am ensnared.
Ethereal flickers softly call,
In the forest night, I lose it all.

Dances of Luminescence in the Gloaming

As the sun dips low, colors blend,
Shades of twilight start to transcend.
Dancing lights in a soft embrace,
Luminescence paints the sky's face.

Fireflies twirl in a joyful spree,
A ballet of dreams, wild and free.
Amidst the trees, a gentle hum,
A symphony where night calls come.

Whispers of dusk in the cooling air,
Each flicker a secret, a tender prayer.
Nature's canvas is brushed anew,
With strokes of light, and shadows too.

Underneath the vast starlit dome,
Creatures awaken, far from home.
The gloaming invites us to play,
In this dance of light, we lose our way.

But as the final rays retreat,
The air thickens with calm and heat.
In this moment, time stands still,
Lost in the magic, a dream fulfilled.

Soft Luminescence of Elfin Dreams

In the quiet realm of misty glade,
Elves whisper secrets, softly played.
Glowing smiles in the twilight stream,
Soft luminescence of purest dream.

Wings flutter lightly, a gentle sound,
Magic encircles, in starlight bound.
Time dances with the shadows where,
Elfin dreams whisper through the air.

Amidst the ferns, a flicker shines,
A tapestry woven with ancient signs.
Through silver leaves, moonlit beams,
Guide us into the realm of dreams.

Echoes of laughter float on the breeze,
Filling the night with enchanted ease.
Holding hands, they spin and twirl,
In luminescent waves, pearls unfurl.

As the world fades into night's embrace,
We chase the spark with gentle grace.
Captured within this dreamlike seam,
Soft luminescence, not quite a dream.

Veils of Light in Whispering Branches

Beneath the arches of the night,
Veils of light dance, a shimmering sight.
Whispering branches sway with ease,
As the wind tells tales through the trees.

Glimmers play upon the forest floor,
A magical realm, inviting more.
Through curtain leaves, shadows glide,
In the woodland's heart, secrets hide.

Each flicker glows, a tender guide,
Leading the lost on a journey wide.
A silver glow in the earthy dark,
Illuminating paths where dreams embark.

The air thickens with silvery sighs,
While starlit wonders fill the skies.
Veils of light twirl in cosmic dance,
Inviting every heart to take a chance.

And as the night begins to fade,
In the glow of dawn, memories are laid.
In whispering branches, we confide,
A journey of light, forever our guide.

The Subtle Dance of Ethereal Lights

Above the world, they glide so free,
Whispers of magic, soft and light.
Stars entwined in a waltz of night,
Painting shadows with silent glee.

Glimmers cast on the ocean's crest,
They twirl and spin in cosmic grace.
Each flicker a story, a hidden place,
A symphony sung by the sun's soft rest.

Embrace the glow that warms the dark,
A soothing balm for weary souls.
In every shimmer, a tale unfolds,
A gentle kiss, a loving spark.

In the stillness of night's embrace,
Dreams take flight where shadows play.
Their essence lingers, night turns to day,
In the dance, we find our place.

So gaze aloft and let them inspire,
The world alight with wonder's glow.
In ethereal realms where spirits flow,
Find the peace that sets hearts afire.

Hushes Beneath the Celestial Dome

Underneath stars, the night breathes slow,
Whispers of secrets in the cool breeze.
Moonlight bathes the world with ease,
A tranquil glow in the twilight's show.

Dreamers drift in a sea of dreams,
The cosmos hums an ancient song.
In this vastness, we all belong,
Finding solace in starlit beams.

Each twinkle holds a wish untold,
Hopes shimmering in the darkened skies.
Hearts entwined, where eternity lies,
A canvas of dreams in colors bold.

Beneath the dome, the world stands still,
The universe whispers its gentle tune.
In shadows cast by the silvery moon,
We dance as one, in love and will.

So let the hush of night enfold,
Our spirits free, our hearts ablaze.
In the quiet, we find our ways,
As stories in starlight unfold.

Crystalline Thoughts in the Forest's Heart

Amongst the trees, where silence reigns,
Whispers of wisdom weave through leaves.
Each breath a journey that never deceives,
Reflections dance in the softest rains.

Crystals shimmer on the forest floor,
Thoughts take form in the morning light.
Nature's secrets are held in sight,
In every shadow, there's something more.

A gentle breeze stirs ancient tales,
Roots entwined in a sacred trust.
In the earth, we find our must,
The quiet strength that never fails.

Amongst the ferns, clarity grows,
Each moment a pearl of insight bright.
With every heartbeat, feel the light,
In crystalline thoughts, the spirit knows.

So wander deep in the woodland's arms,
Where nature sings its soft refrain.
In the heart of the forest, break every chain,
In peace and stillness, embrace its charms.

Flickers of Enchantment on Silent Paths

On winding trails where shadows weave,
Magic twinkles in the night air.
Every step holds a promise rare,
In the stillness, our hearts believe.

With every flicker, a tale unfolds,
Whispers of wonder guide our way.
In moonlit dances, we choose to stay,
As mysteries wrapped in night's soft folds.

Beneath the stars, we light the way,
In the echoes of laughter, love ignites.
With dreams we gather in soft moonlights,
Together we wander, come what may.

Through enchanted woods, we find our song,
In every rustle, a heartbeat shared.
The journey onward, a bond declared,
Embracing moments where we belong.

So walk the paths where magic swirls,
Each flicker a guide through the unseen.
In the quiet, find what has always been,
Love's gentle whisper in a world that twirls.

Delicate Glimmers in the Heart of Stillness

Amidst the whispering trees, where shadows lay,
Soft glimmers dance, inviting night to stay.
A breath of silence fills the waiting air,
Each flicker speaks of secrets laid bare.

In twilight's arms, the stars begin to rise,
Their shimmering tales twinkle in the skies.
A tranquil heart finds solace in the glow,
As time unfurls, each moment flows slow.

Petals of dreams drift gently on the breeze,
Cradled by stillness, wrapped in soft unease.
Reflections shimmer in a silver stream,
Awakening whispers of a distant dream.

Every heartbeat pulses with the night,
Painted in hues of amber, soft and bright.
The mind surrenders to the soft allure,
In stillness, find a timeless, tranquil cure.

Delicate glimmers weave through open hearts,
Binding the dreams with invisible arts.
In the heart of stillness, beauty finds a way,
To linger softly, never to decay.

Hidden Currents of Luminary Essence

Beneath the surface, a vibrant flow,
Currents of light in darkness glow.
Secrets whisper in ethereal grace,
Their luminous dance, a shimmering trace.

Stars unravel tales in cosmic seas,
Each flicker ignites forgotten keys.
In shadows deep, the bright beats reside,
Where night unfolds, and dreams abide.

Every heartbeat echoes with soft light,
Guiding the lost through the veils of night.
Hidden currents weave through silent dreams,
Carrying stories on moonlit beams.

The essence of hopes floats in the air,
A symphony played with colors rare.
In the quietude, intuition takes flight,
Chasing the spark that ignites the night.

With every breath, a promise is born,
Hidden currents in the soul's early morn.
Luminary whispers shimmer and weave,
In the heart of darkness, we learn to believe.

Enchanted Gleams Beneath the Canopy

Beneath the emerald leaves, shadows play,
Whispers of magic in the light's soft sway.
Gleams of enchantment dance on the ground,
Each moment, a treasure waiting to be found.

Sunbeams cascade, embracing the earth,
Filling the air with a sense of rebirth.
In the quiet rustle, secrets unfold,
Wrapped in the warmth of stories untold.

Fragrant blooms offer their gentle cheer,
While the world hums, inviting us near.
With every step, the soul starts to glow,
In this enchanted realm, time's currents flow.

Reflections of dreams in the puddles lie,
Caught in the gaze of the dappled sky.
Magic exists in the simple and small,
In the canvas of nature, there's wonder for all.

In the canopy's embrace, hearts intertwine,
Lost in the beauty, bodies align.
Enchanted gleams whisper true and clear,
Under the trees, we gather all fear.

Dreaming in Light's Embrace

In the dawn's cradle, dreams start to rise,
Wrapped in warmth beneath the waking skies.
Every ray weaves stories, soft and bright,
Bathing the world in the glow of light.

Whispers of morning dance on the stream,
Carrying spirits like a tender dream.
In each gentle flutter, hearts ignite,
As they unfurl beneath the glowing light.

Soft visions drift, illuminating the mind,
A tapestry woven, colors aligned.
The day's embrace holds the deepest grace,
In the warmth of hope, we find our place.

With every heartbeat, light flows and weaves,
Binding our souls to the shifts in the leaves.
In this sacred space, shadows recede,
As we follow the path where our spirits lead.

Dreaming in light's embrace, fear melts away,
In the radiant glow, we find our way.
Together we wander, spirits set free,
In the dawn's tender light, just you and me.

Whispers Among Ancient Roots

Beneath the canopy, secrets dwell,
The whispers of ages in stories they tell.
Twisting and turning, the roots intertwine,
In the heart of the forest, where shadows align.

Moss-covered graves where old spirits sleep,
Guarding the wisdom that they've vowed to keep.
Echoes of laughter float on the breeze,
In harmony with rustling branches and trees.

The dance of the fireflies, a flickering sight,
Guiding lost souls in the depth of the night.
Each breath of the breeze tells a tale once known,
Of moments long gone, yet never alone.

With every soft rustle, a gentle embrace,
The songs of the ancients merge with the space.
Here in the silence, the past finds a voice,
In whispers among roots, we all have the choice.

The Unseen Glow of Time's Embrace

In shadows of twilight, time whispers low,
Its unseen glow wraps the world in a flow.
Moments unwritten dance in the night,
As silence unveils the echoes of light.

Each tick of the clock, a story unfolds,
A tapestry woven with threads of pure gold.
In the depths of the stillness, a heartbeat remains,
Counting the dreams, the joys, and the pains.

Under the stars, time drapes its gray shawl,
Enveloping all with a soft, silent call.
The whispers of ages caress the old stone,
In the arms of the cosmos, we're never alone.

As morning awakes, the past starts to fade,
Yet the essence lingers in memories stayed.
In the gentle embrace of both dusk and dawn,
Time leaves its glow, forever withdrawn.

Shimmers in the Dawn's Pastel Wings

As dawn breaks the silence, the sky starts to blush,
In pastels of pink where the world feels a hush.
Wings of the morning dance through the air,
Brushing the treetops with delicate care.

The shimmer of sunlight spills over the glade,
A palette of colors in nature's parade.
Softly it beckons the creatures to play,
Inviting the world to embrace a new day.

In each trembling petal, a promise resides,
The whisper of hope in the gentle tides.
Butterflies flutter, painting dreams on the breeze,
As laughter of children chases shadows of trees.

With every new dawn, the past is reborn,
In shimmers of beauty, the heart feels the scorn.
Yet all is forgiven in morning's soft light,
As pastel wings usher the magic of night.

The Gentle Caress of Leafy Shadows

Beneath sprawling branches, the coolness resides,
Where whispers of nature in stillness confides.
Leafy shadows dance in a muted ballet,
Embracing the wanderer who's lost on the way.

In sun-dappled moments, the world halts to breathe,
The soft touch of green like a tapestry weaves.
In the heart of the forest, peace lingers near,
As darkness and light blend, crafting all we hold dear.

Each rustle of leaves tells a tale from the past,
Of loves that once flourished, and friendships to last.
The gentle caress of the shadows above,
Reminds us of life, its lessons, and love.

In the quiet embrace of the leafy retreat,
The soul finds a rhythm with nature's heartbeat.
Here time is a circle, the seasons entwine,
In the gentle caress, we're forever divine.

The Fleeting Essence of Gossamer Wings

In the quiet of twilight's embrace,
A whisper of color takes flight.
Delicate threads in a dance of grace,
Gossamer dreams flutter in light.

Moments like raindrops, they shimmer and fade,
Caught in the net of time's gentle spin.
Ephemeral beauty in shadows laid,
Life's fleeting essence wrapped softly within.

Wings weave through soft, echoing sighs,
A tapestry spun with laughter and tears.
Underneath starlit and watchful skies,
Each flicker of joy counters lingering fears.

With each beat, speaks the heart's tender song,
Tales of the brave and the broken alike.
In the breeze, echoes where we belong,
Gossamer threads in the night sky strike.

As dawn unfolds, a new day draws near,
Wings clutch the morning, a soft, bright plume.
Memories linger in petals of sheer,
In silence, life whispers, ready to bloom.

Secrets Whirl Around Ancient Oaks

Whispering winds tell tales of old,
Where shadows stretch long in the dusk.
Time wraps the roots in stories untold,
Secrets of nature, revealing their husk.

Beneath the branches, soft whispers dwell,
Each leaf a page in history's tome.
In the heart of the woods, nature's spell,
Cradles the tales of travelers' roam.

Moss carpets the ground, where footprints fade,
Echoes of laughter, of love once shared.
Among the giants, memories parade,
In stillness, the essence of lives declared.

Ancient oaks hold the stories of time,
Their limbs a throne for the winds to play.
Nature's verses, in rhythm and rhyme,
Guarding the secrets, come what may.

Under the boughs, when the moonlight gleams,
Love dances with shadows, a timeless trance.
Night weaves its fabric with silken dreams,
In the heart of the forest, lost in a glance.

Dreams Unfurling in the Dewy Dawn

Softly the light breaks through misty gloom,
Awakening petals that shimmer and glow.
Each breath of morning whispers a bloom,
Dreams unfurl in soft waves, gentle and slow.

Crimson and gold, the colors entwine,
Nature unfurls its delicate art.
In the cradle of day, new hopes align,
With each tender moment, a fresh start.

Beneath the sky, where the meadow sways,
Time dances lightly, no weight to be found.
Melodies twirl in the sun's warm rays,
Dreams take flight on the soft, fertile ground.

A chorus of nature, in harmony sings,
Echoing promises through the wide expanse.
In the heart of the dawn, life gently clings,
To a symphony crafted from hope and chance.

As the day beckons, with laughter and light,
Lingering moments bring joy's sweet embrace.
In the dew of the dawn, all feels just right,
Dreams unfurl gently, captured in grace.

Echoes of Luminous Fancies

In the twilight glow where shadows play,
Fancies rise like whispers of night.
Each twinkle a memory, fading away,
Echoes of dreams taking flight.

Stars paint the canvas, a silvery hue,
Where laughter and longing entwined.
In the depths of silence, love's secrets accrue,
Tales of the heart, softly divined.

Beneath the vast expanse, wishes unfurl,
Like ribbons of starlight, woven with care.
In moonlit shadows, emotions swirl,
Echoes of promise drift softly in air.

The night holds a mirror, reflecting our fears,
Yet glimmers of hope dance in the dark.
Through every heartbeat, despite all the tears,
Luminous fancies ignite the spark.

As dawn edges in, the magic may fade,
Yet dreams linger softly, awaiting the call.
In echoes of laughter, memories made,
A tapestry woven, uniting us all.

Murmurs of Time in the Hearth's Embrace

In the flicker of fire, shadows dance,
Whispers of stories, a timeless romance.
Embers glow softly, secrets they share,
Echoes of laughter, memories rare.

The hearth holds warmth, a comforting light,
Crackling tales woven, both day and night.
In the stillness, hearts find their way,
Guided by flickers, no words to say.

Time drips like honey, sweet and slow,
Each moment cherished, like soft winter snow.
In the glow of the flame, a gentle sigh,
Murmurs of time, beneath the vast sky.

Through the ashes, treasures remain,
Stories of love, of joy, and of pain.
Fires will flicker, but hearts they will bind,
In the hearth's embrace, solace we find.

So gather around, let the tales flow,
In the warm hearth's glow, let memories grow.
As time softly murmurs, in flickers it flows,
In the hearth's sweet embrace, eternity glows.

Shimmers of Dust in the Hidden Hollow

In the twilight glow, where secrets lie,
Dust motes shimmer, as soft winds sigh.
A hidden hollow, draped in pure bliss,
Nature's whispers tell stories amiss.

Among ancient trees, green and profound,
Life's delicate echoes can be found.
A world so quiet, yet vibrant and whole,
Shimmers of dust, igniting the soul.

Underneath moonlight, the shadows play,
In the hidden hollow, night turns to day.
Glimmers of memories drift through the air,
Each shimmer a dance, a joy we can share.

Flowing like water, soft whispers thread,
Through the boughs and leaves, gently spread.
Nature's tapestry, woven with grace,
Shimmers of dust, a lovely embrace.

In these quiet moments, the heart can explore,
The beauty of life, forever in store.
Through shimmers of dust, the stories will flow,
In the hidden hollow, treasures will grow.

A Quiet Awakening of Age-Old Tales

In the hush of dawn, where shadows unfold,
Age-old tales whisper, secrets retold.
Mornings awaken with stories anew,
In the quiet of time, dreams come into view.

Beneath ancient boughs, where dreams take flight,
Echoes of laughter linger into the night.
A gentle breeze carries words from the past,
Awakening whispers, forever to last.

As sun kisses earth, a symphony plays,
Notes of remembrance dance in soft rays.
With each break of dawn, life starts to spin,
A quiet awakening, where dreams begin.

In the dappling light, stories entwined,
The heart holds each moment, tenderly aligned.
The past and the present in harmony flow,
Awakening quietly, as the seasons bestow.

So listen closely, as the world comes alive,
In the stillness of morn, where wonders thrive.
A quiet awakening, forever it trails,
In the hearts of the dreamers, are age-old tales.

The Silken Threads of Destiny

In the tapestry woven, fate finds its way,
Silken threads shimmer, in night and in day.
Every strand crafted, with purpose so clear,
Binding our journeys, both far and near.

Through labyrinthine paths, destiny weaves,
Whispers of fortune, in hearts it believes.
Each thread a milestone, a crossroad defined,
In the fabric of life, our dreams intertwined.

With flickers of hope, we soar and we dive,
Holding the threads that help us survive.
In the loom of existence, we create and mend,
The silken threads twine, as stories blend.

Time moves like yarn, soft and unspooled,
Each twist and each turn, by passion fueled.
Through highs and through lows, the patterns emerge,
With silken threads, our destinies surge.

So cherish each thread, both fragile and strong,
For in life's design, we all play along.
The silken threads weave, in harmony's song,
In the fabric of fate, where we all belong.

www.ingramcontent.com/pod-product-compliance
Ingram Content Group UK Ltd.
Pitfield, Milton Keynes, MK11 3LW, UK
UKHW021639200125
4187UKWH00003B/190